Jack Signs!

WRITTEN BY KAREN HARDWICKE
ILLUSTRATED BY AMANDA WALKER

LEARN ALONG WITH ME!

WHENEVER YOU SEE THIS BADGE, YOU CAN HEAD OVER TO

avidlanguage.com/jack-signs

TO LEARN SOME SIGNS AND SEE MY WHOLE STORY SIGNED!

Taken from a diary dated 2nd February 1998, when Jack was 2 years, 2 months.

Today, I decided to give Jack more signs - so he's got something to give back.
Feel like it's unfair to deny him this.
<u>Relief</u> at this decision.
It's a big strain to try and get speech all the time.

So, this is our story…

Picture a little boy whose name is Jack.
A little boy with sparkly blue eyes and hair the colour of the sun.
A little boy with two hearing aids that don't quite sit behind his ears, but stick out, like this:

Jack is learning to listen,
but he has no words.

Well, apart from one...

'NO!'

'**No**' is a very useful word.

It is useful when it's time for nursery.

Can you see Jack's mummy
standing at the door with his coat?
Can you see her pointing to a
photograph of his nursery on the wall?

Jack lies down on the floor,
shouting **'NO!'** as loudly as he can.

It is useful at other times too.

Here is Mummy, shopping bags
balanced on the back of her buggy.
The sun is shining. It is good.

Jack has been collecting sticks from the
Abbey grounds. So many sticks Jack
can barely carry them.

He is proud of his sticks.

Mummy does not want the sticks to be
brought inside. She asks Jack to leave
them in the garden.

Jack lies down in the street,
shouting '**NO!**' as loudly as he can,
his face puckered and red.

Mummy looks up and down the street
and waits for him to stop.

'**No**' is useful when it is sunny but useful when it is snowing too.

Here are Mummy, Caitlin and Jack on their way to the shops. It's getting dark and Caitlin is hungry.
Did you notice that Mummy has lost a glove?

Jack is wandering through the snow. It is fun to catch the flakes in his mittens!

'Come on, Jack!' calls Mummy.

Jack lies on his back in the snow, spreads his arms and legs wide and shouts,

'NO, NO, NO!'

(He is **not** a snow angel.)

Mummy walks more quickly and hopes that Jack will follow.

15th December 1997

Jack has tantrums several times a day. I try to ignore them and sometimes put him on the 'naughty step' but then I feel worse.

When 'no' is a battle and Mummy is tired and Jack is tired too, Mummy does something new.

She finds a book of signs.

Let's take a look, shall we?

Mummy takes Jack into the street and shows him a car. Jack likes cars. She looks at the book and signs 'car'.

Jack copies the sign. Mummy laughs and Jack laughs too! And the sun comes out in the street.

This was the first time.

Here is Jack at breakfast time.
Jack is thirsty. He is signing 'milk'!

Do you know what is happening here?

Mummy is teaching Jack the sign for 'slow'. They have found as many snails as they can and have let them go!

Here are Jack and Caitlin. Curled up on the sofa and munching Skittles that are the colour of happiness.

Jack would like more but Mummy signs 'all gone'.

Jack throws himself onto the carpet and kicks his legs with fury.

Sometimes, signs are not enough.

Little by little, Jack learns to share his thoughts.

One day, Mummy and Jack go for a walk. They pass a woman who is sleeping in the sunshine.

'Look!' signs Jack, pointing with a shocked look on his face. 'Lady DEAD!'

'Come on, Jack!' replies Mummy
with some awkwardness,
'Let's go home now.'

Mummy smiles at the woman
and shuffles quickly on.

So, here is Jack.
A little boy with eyes that sparkle
and hair the colour of the sun.
A little boy with two hearing aids that
now sit nicely behind his ears.
A little boy who knows more than a hundred signs!
Jack is happy and Mummy is happy too.

4th April 1999
Now Jack has around 100 signs and he has started to build sentences:
'Tomorrow, Baba (Mummy), Ca Ca (Caitlin), Gack (Jack!) toy shop.'
'Tomorrow, when Baba, Ca Ca, Gack wake up - bic bics!'

This isn't the end of our story.

In fact, it is just the beginning.

ABOUT THE AUTHOR

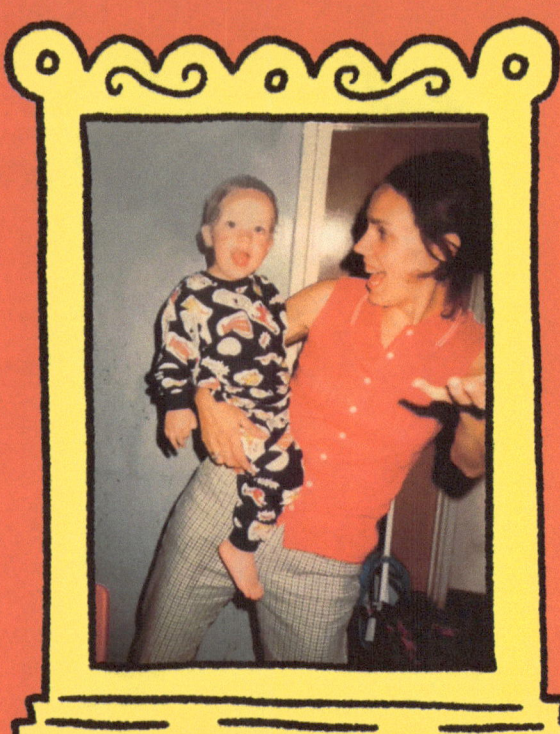

Karen Hardwicke is the parent of a young deaf adult and has been a Teacher of the Deaf for over ten years. She enjoys the 3 Rs: reading, writing and (fair weather) running. She loves using Music with deaf children and composing slightly rubbish songs at the drop of a hat.

'Jack Signs!' is a story about a deaf child, his hearing sister and their Mum. It is an ode to Sign Language, which changed their family's life.

other books by Karen

ABOUT THE ILLUSTRATOR

Amanda Walker is an illustrator and artist from Berkshire, UK. As well as illustrating colouring and children's books, she enjoys painting and making quilts - but doesn't like parting with any of them. She has a large collection of paintings and quilts. You can have a look at more of her lovely work @mannyjeann on Instagram!

for Jack, Cait and Jamie... "This is living, this is." - K.H.

JACK SIGNS! Published by AVID Language Ltd, 3 Cam Drive, Ely CB6 2WH, UK. First published in 2022.
ISBN: Paperback: 978-1-913968-15-1   **Hardcover:** 978-1-913968-16-8
Text copyright: ©Karen Hardwicke 2022   Illustrations copyright ©Amanda Walker 2022
Author photograph ©Karen Hardwicke   Editing and layout by Tanya Saunders for AVID Language Ltd.
All rights reserved.

www.avidlanguage.com/books

www.ingramcontent.com/pod-product-compliance
Lightning Source LLC
Chambersburg PA
CBHW050756110526
44588CB00002B/21